T0387481

HEALTHY HABITS

RESTING

by Emma Carlson Berne

Consultant: Beth Gambro
Reading Specialist, Yorkville, Illinois

Minneapolis, Minnesota

Teaching Tips

Before Reading

- Look at the cover of the book. Discuss the picture and the title.

- Ask readers to brainstorm a list of what they already know about resting. What can they expect to see in the book?

- Go on a picture walk, looking through the pictures to discuss vocabulary and make predictions about the text.

During Reading

- Read for purpose. Encourage readers to think about resting habits as they are reading.

- Ask readers to look for the details of the book. What are they learning about different ways to rest?

- If readers encounter an unknown word, ask them to look at the sounds in the word. Then, ask them to look at the rest of the page. Are there any clues to help them understand?

After Reading

- Encourage readers to pick a buddy and reread the book together.

- Ask readers to name two things that can make resting a habit. Find the pages that tell about these things.

- Ask readers to write or draw something they learned about resting.

Credits:
Cover and title page, © Africa Studio/Shutterstock; 3, © New Africa/Adobe Stock; 5, © Africa Studio/Adobe Stock; 7, © be free/iStock; 8–9, © Geber86/iStock; 11, © Africa Studio/Adobe Stock; 12–13, © ulkas/Adobe Stock, © Andrii Bezvershenko/Shutterstock; 15, © zhenya/Adobe Stock; 16–17, ©Amorn Suriyan/iStock; 18–19, © FatCamera/iStock; 20–21, © AaronAmat/iStock; 22T, © Sinseeho/Shutterstock; 22M, © MementoImage/iStock; 22B, © Africa Studio/Shutterstock; 23TL, © Nina/peopleimages.com/Adobe Stock; 23TM, © Chutima Chaochaiya/Shutterstock; 23TR, © DragonImages/Adobe Stock; 23BL, © JJAVA/Adobe Stock; 23BR, © Pixel-Shot/Adobe Stock.

STATEMENT ON USAGE OF GENERATIVE ARTIFICIAL INTELLIGENCE
Bearport Publishing remains committed to publishing high-quality nonfiction books. Therefore, we restrict the use of generative AI to ensure accuracy of all text and visual components pertaining to a book's subject. See BearportPublishing.com for details.

Library of Congress Cataloging-in-Publication Data

Names: Berne, Emma Carlson, 1979- author.
Title: Resting / Emma Carlson Berne ; consultant, Beth Gambro, Reading
    Specialist, Yorkville, Illinois.
Description: Minneapolis, Minnesota : Bearport Publishing Company, [2024] |
    Series: Healthy habits | Includes bibliographical references and index.
Identifiers: LCCN 2023028232 (print) | LCCN 2023028233 (ebook) | ISBN
    9798889162438 (library binding) | ISBN 9798889162506 (paperback) | ISBN
    9798889162568 (ebook)
Subjects: LCSH: Rest--Juvenile literature.
Classification: LCC RA785 .B4835 2024 (print) | LCC RA785 (ebook) | DDC
    612.7/6--dc23/eng/20230710
LC record available at https://lccn.loc.gov/2023028232
LC ebook record available at https://lccn.loc.gov/2023028233

Copyright © 2024 Bearport Publishing Company. All rights reserved. No part of this publication may be reproduced in whole or in part, stored in any retrieval system, or transmitted in any form or by any means, electronic, mechanical, photocopying, recording, or otherwise, without written permission from the publisher.
For more information, write to Bearport Publishing, 5357 Penn Avenue South, Minneapolis, MN 55419.

Contents

Yawn! 4

Make It a Habit 22

Glossary 23

Index 24

Read More 24

Learn More Online. 24

About the Author 24

I open my eyes in the morning.

Blink, blink!

I had a good night's sleep.

Now, I am ready for my day.

Taking time to rest is good for me.

I do it every day.

That makes it a healthy **habit**!

During the day, I love to run and play.

Moving is good for my body.

My **muscles** work hard.

At the end of the day, I am tired.

So, I sleep every night.

This helps my body **recover**.

Zzzz!

Sleep helps my brain, too.

My brain uses the time to make **memories**.

Sometimes, it works out problems during sleep.

Getting enough sleep is important.

It is good to go to bed on time.

I get about 10 hours of rest every night.

15

Sometimes, I get tired during the day.

So, I take a nap.

This short sleep gives me extra **energy**.

I can also rest while I am awake.

Quiet time lets me take a break.

It helps me stay calm during a busy day.

I feel great when I get rest.

Every day I take care of my body this way.

It is a healthy habit!

Make It a Habit

A habit is something you do every day. What are ways we can make resting a habit?

Try to go to bed and get up at the same time each day.

Can't fall asleep? Try reading a book or writing in a journal.

If you get tired during the day, give yourself a rest break.

Glossary

energy the power to do things, such as work or run

habit something done regularly

memories things from the past that the brain can remember

muscles parts of the body that help you move

recover to get better

Index

energy 16
habit 6, 20, 22
memories 12
nap 16
problems 12
recover 10
rest 6, 14, 19–20, 22
sleep 4, 10, 12, 14, 16, 22

Read More

Chang, Kirsten. *Getting Sleep (A Healthy Life).* Minneapolis: Bellwether Media, 2022.

Connors, Kathleen. *I Get My Rest! (Healthy Me!).* New York: Gareth Stevens Publishing, 2023.

Learn More Online

1. Go to **www.factsurfer.com** or scan the QR code below.
2. Enter **"Healthy Habits Resting"** into the search box.
3. Click on the cover of this book to see a list of websites.

About the Author

Emma Carlson Berne lives with her family in Cincinnati, Ohio. She loves going to bed early.